IN MY VIEW

TABLE OF CONTENT

1. India and England dream — page 2
2. Who will start the war – Armageddon — page 3
3. Church Dream – Woman of Zion — page 4
4. Son that best suit the White Race — page 4 - 6
5. Book of Malachi deciphered — page 6 - 10
6. God's Saving — page 11 - 14
7. Plea to God — page 15 - 16
8. In My View — page 17 - 20
9. My Concern — page 21 - 28
10. Worst Disasters — page 29
11. In Our Land — page 30 - 32
12. Jamaica Dream — page 33
13. Muscle Spasm — page 34
14. Iceland, Justin Trudeau, John Travolta's Wife Dream+ — page 35 - 37
15. More Death + — page 38 - 41
16. Old Testament of the Bible — page 42
17. Vladimir Putin and Donald Trump Dream — page 43
18. Common, Shaq, Queen Latifah Dream — page 44 - 47
19. Jack Hill Protocol Dream — page 48
20. Stop Talking — page 49 - 50
21. Books by Michelle Jean — page 51

IN MY VIEW

The craziness of this world – people of this world is something else. Wow to my dream world. My dreams are truly beyond me. Just this morning I dreamt England. I was at this show – show to do with Black People. This Black Gentleman was taking pictures and I wanted to take a picture with him, and I did. I used my tablet to takes pictures of him and with him. In the dream he was far away but I got close to him and took the pictures. After that, I was walking with this Young Black Girl. Seeing my surroundings in England, all I saw was concrete buildings – tall. This one building of concrete and glass was like a square box going up. You know what. Think of the tallest residential structure in India that the richest man in that country made for himself, and his family.

I did not like the building. For some, the building would be beautiful but to me, it was ugly. Looking around, you did not see many people. All I saw was a Muslim Family; I think they were Black and or, of Somalian heritage in their habitat – home. Then I saw this 1(one) Black Female. She was prostrating to the ground. Meaning, she was in a prostrating position on the ground and or, floor praying in her habitat – home.

Continuing to walk, I saw this White Worm – different type of worm and I made a comment about how the insects of England were different.

Walking on I saw this symbol; Babylonian Symbol on the ground. I cannot tell you fully what the symbol was. But the outer shell was circular – round, and of brassy gold. I cannot tell you what the inside symbol look like. I was not focussing on the symbol. I told the Young Black Girl that was with me who had a shaved head, but on the top part of her head, her hair was brassy gold that; **<u>Blacks were not to marry Babylonians.</u>** She said, she knew but; despite her knowing the truth of Blacks not being permitted to and or, not allowed to marry Babylonians with Babylonians being Indians, she was upset at me.

I will not fully analyze this dream because I truly do not know the symbol that was on the ground in England.

I do not know if any Earthquake is going to rock England, or if further unrest is going to be on land where Muslims blow up places in that land. Nor do I know what is going to happen in India land wise – tsunami – earthquake wise. I just have to watch and see what happens.

Little by little war is going to be on land.

WORLD WAR 4
ARMAGEDDON
THE WAR OF NATIONS

I know prior to this dream - around the beginning of July if not earlier; ***I did dream America going to war. They; America was the one to start war.*** This is absolutely nothing new for me when it comes to this land. Other nations must bow to their bully tactics, and the rest of the inept politicians of the globe side with this destructive, and warmonger land. A land that has and have put the entire globe on the Docket of Death, and in debt with death. Therefore; many lands, and the people of those lands are scheduled to die; going to die. This, humans can blame self for. We were taught.

"THOU SHALT NOT KILL"

Yet, in the wake of Life; no not life; Death, you have politicians globally going against life by sending our children - well some of your children on the Battlefield of Death to kill. Thus, many humans globally - well all those who are in the Global Armies of Death are paid assassins. They defy life therefore, God cannot be with these people, nor can God be with their families. These people knowingly, and willingly defy life - the direct order and or, a direct order of God.

No one can defend Earth. Earth need no defense from humans because Earth can defend herself. It is humans that destroy Earth therefore, Earth need to get rid of humans - evict humans from in her. Thus, Earth need defense against humans in the sense of sins. And I know this wording will not make any sense to some, but it makes sense to me.

Earth can no longer defend humans. Meaning, continue to give evil - evil and wicked humans, and spirits a home in her.

We know the White Race know not Life or God. This is why they; the White Race lie; use their lying and deceitful bible to trap the different nations so that they end up in hell with them.

Thus, humans have and has forgotten about *GOOD AND EVIL.*

A nation of vipers that knoweth not God; the True God of Life, cannot speak of life, or educate you about life. All they can do is kill you because Sin and or, Death is all they know.

You cannot say God said, then paint God as a giver backer taker.
A God that break the very laws we are given to uphold; keep.

Life is not Death therefore, as humans we need to know the difference between the Children and People of Life, and the Children and People of Death.

We as the Children and People of Life know what Life and Death is all about therefore, as the Children and People of Life; God, we need to; have to do all to live right, walk right, talk right, separate ourselves from the Devil's true own, and more.

We cannot say we are of Life; God, and live amongst the dysfunctional of Life. Those who care not for self; their Spiritual Life. We know **OUR TRUE SPIRITUAL LIFE IS SEPARATED FROM OUR PHYSICAL LIFE.** Yes, in a human sense our spirit is joined to the flesh, but in the truest sense, LIFE AND DEATH ARE SEPARATED. Meaning, those who are of life is separated from those who are of Death. And yes, my explanation is confusing to you, but I truly do not know how to put my wording for you to comprehend. Therefore, if you have not comprehension on a higher level; life, you will not comprehend, over stand, or understand what I am trying to teach you.

Did I dream about the bible?

Yes. Therefore, I have to read Malachi. I cannot disobey my order anymore.

Did I dream about me being in Church?

Yes.

I was in the Church of the Woman of Zion.

I will not get too much into the dream. All I can tell you is that the Woman of Zion had Cancer. She was happy to see me. She hugged me, and I gave her a tree; small Tree of Life in hopes that the tree could cure her Cancer. Therefore, Black Zion need to clean itself up, and get rid of the Cancers that is affecting it; Zion.

True Zionites must separate them self from the fake ones that say they are of Zion but are truly not. They just use Zion for their monetary gain; profit. They have not site to see yet, fool people with false hope.

We; the True People of Zion can no longer cause Zion pain. We need to live. So yes, I am going to read Malachi and see, and if I can decipher this book, I will decipher it for you. You need to know the truth, because we cannot continue on down the wrong path of the White Race.

It's time humans learn to respect God. And yes, I am still dreaming about the decimation of Earth weather wise.

JAH LIVE – Robert Nesta Marley aka, Bob Marley
JAH LIVE – Luciano the reggae artist

So yes, the truth is an offense for those who refuse the truth. Thus, the wicked and evil cannot, and will never ever accept their wrongs. To them, their wrongs are right which is so sad on their part. Therefore, the wicked and evil will never be able to attain life. They know not God, the truth.

Listen, ABSOLUTELY NO ONE CAN OUTLIVE LIFE, NOR CAN ANYONE OUTLIVE DEATH IF THEIR NAME IS IN THE BOOK OF DEATH.

However, if your name is in the Book of Life you can outlive Death.

Right now, as to what is happening in the world today due to chemical, and germ warfare by the white Race. *GUILTINESS by the great Robert Nesta Marley aka, Bob Marley* best fit the White Race Globally. This race is truly guilty of genocide therefore, they (the White Race) do all for

Death. This race in My View hath no conscience therefore, they lie and deceive; kill everywhere they go. It matters not if their killing is lies and deceit, false education, their unjust and unfair judicial, and corporate systems, their lying and false religions they use to get you the different races to bow down to so that you can; will lose your place in life, the wars they knowingly, and willingly create to keep strife amongst the different races of the globe so that God cannot come into Earth, the racial injustice they instigate, the sexual confusion that they manufacture to let you sin sexually, and more.

So yes, the White Race are humanities Down Pressers therefore, "they eat the Bread of Sorrow, and Sad Tomorrow."

Therefore, evil; the White Race cannot have a conscience because their living is false, truly unclean; dirty. Like I said in my previous book. **NO ONE HAVE TO LIVE THE WHITE MAN'S WAY – DEATH'S WAY.**

Listen, we all have a choice to live clean. It is us as humans that ignore God and live the dirty way – Death's way. Death truly love it when humans sin. When humans sin, the more time Death has to live and yes, kill.

GOD CANNOT SAVE THE UNCLEAN. GOD MUST SAVE THE CLEAN ONLY.

NOR WOULD GOD ALLOW THE CHILDREN AND PEOPLE OF LIFE TO SAVE THE CHILDREN AND PEOPLE OF DEATH.

Many in the White Race need a saving grace we all know this, but I refuse to allow God to save them – the wicked and evil of this race; the White Race no matter the hue. And yes, I need to talk about the ONE DROP RULE when it comes to Blood – Genetics.

Absolutely no one Black should die to save you or save you period. Save the White Race based on hue and evil deeds.

You've; the White Race lied on God.

Took many in life (the physical and spiritual realm) from God then want the ones you've deceived to save you!!!!

Kick rocks and bare your own punishment in hell because, **all the happenings here on Earth did not have to be.**

No Death can have life period. If you in the White Race wanted life, you would have lived good and true. Lived a good and true life here on Earth.

You cannot have unfair and unjust laws for the different nations and think God; the God of Life would stand with you with your evils.

You cannot give people pork to eat and think Life would not be against you. Cast you out of life.

Life is worth it. It is you in the White Race that truly do not know this. Hence, I cannot worry about humans globally because shortly all must come to an end for the wicked and evil of Earth.

Absolutely no one can have true peace without knowing the truth of God.

Without truth you cannot live, you can only die. Therefore, we were told "TRUTH IS EVERLASTING LIFE."

Thus, *your EVERLASTING LIFE if not dependent on God, it is dependent on you the individual.*

Michelle
July 7, 2020

And yes, I did read the Book of Malachi July 7th, 2020. After reading this book this is what I wrote.

"Book of Malachi"

God do not corrupt
God do not curse

Once you walk away from God that is it. God leave you to your heart's desire. As for the churches, God is with none.

God do not ordain any church or oversee any. Therefore, no priest or pastor is of God.

Judah is no more. Was deemed unclean. The windows and doors of God is closed to Judah because Judah made it so.

God did walk away from Israel because the Children of Israel did marry the Children of Babylon hence, forfeiting life. Therefore, God could not command Malachi.

Malachi is false. God cannot love one child over the next because God do not play favorites – favoritism.

God is just
God is right
God is truth
God is true life

The burdens of man are the burdens of man.
The lies of men are the lies of men.

God cannot corrupt your seed.

Once God has deemed a nation unclean, they are unclean forever, and the Children and People of God cannot enter those unclean lands. It is more than categorically forbidden for the Children and People of God to enter any unclean land – place.

God do not give anyone anything unclean. It is us as humans that give unclean including, give God unclean prayers, unclean churches, unclean mosques, unclean temples, and more to go in. Thus, God do not go into unclean places, or homes.

This is also why God cannot come into Earth because Earth is truly unclean.

See the:

Wars of men

Religious wars
Racism
Hate
Humans sacrificing humans
Humans killing humans

The sin and sins of each human here on Earth, and more.

So yes, earth must pay; be ravaged by fire and water.

The punishment of Earth has absolutely nothing to do with God but, has all to do with us as humans. We made Earth a wasteland.

We caused Earth to become a cesspool of Sin and Death.

We as humans corrupted our Physical Home – Earth, not God. Instead of keeping true to life, many kept true to Death.

We as humans made Death rich off us.

Many if not all were/was not taught the penalty associated to/with 1 sin therefore, Death became our plague; Cancer Stick here on Earth.

As humans, we cannot blame God for our demise; we have to blame self.

I've told you in other books, God did not sin for us, we sinned for self.

We have to bare the burdens; penalty for our wrongs; sins.

The righteous – Children and People of Life cannot face the judgement of Death because their life is secure with Life; God. The judgement is for all those who have not life. Meaning, their name is in the Book of Death. Thus, having more sin on their Sin record than Good.

If you do not know God, how can God know you?

If you have no savings with God, how can God save you?

If all you give God is unclean, how can God save you?

If you have more Bad than Good, how can God save you?

If you do all the wrongs in the world, why should God bow down to Death and sacrifice a Child of Life; Anyone of Life for that matter to save you?

You did not think of your life; soul so, why should God think of your life and soul for you?

So yes, the Wicked and Evil must pay for their sins. They cannot escape their judgement, nor would Death allow anyone on the Docket of Death to go free.

I've told you in other books that; Death protect Life – God. It is Death that keep the Wicked and Evil of this Earth, and the Spiritual Realm away from God – Life.

Absolutely no one evil have or can get an audience with God.

What belongs to Death belong to Death.

What belongs to Life belong to Life.

In the truest sense, and form, God know not Death because God did not create Death. It is us as humans that created our own Hell – Death. See your sin and sins. Tally them (your sins) up, and you will know your hell.

Tally up your good as well.

How many Good do you have verses Evil?

Listen, if God was our true guide, and worth; the Earth would not be riddled in sin.

Yes, billions say they praise God, worship God, but it is Death they praise and worship without knowing it.

Many say fear God, but I say unto you; truly love God, respect God, and be truthful to God.

God do not want or need people to fear him.

God requires truth. True love and respect.

When you truly love God then life opens up to you.
You are at true peace.
You are not as sick.

Fear brings on sickness.
Stress
Hate
Panic, and more.

Therefore, know God, and truly love God.

IN MY VIEW

So yes, I am truly glad that the time is up for the Wicked and Evil of Earth, and the Spiritual Realm.

I am also happy – truly happy that God will not save the Wicked and Evil. It's time for true life to live, and manifest here on Earth.

Satan's Day is up. Now life – Good and True Life must remain; live in true peace, and void of the ills, and pain of Death – all evil.

The New Testament of Man must never manifest Lovey.

No one Black or anyone for that matter should or must be sacrificed to save the White Race.

Lovey, you and I know Death cannot save anyone. Death can only kill you. But then, Black Jesus did sacrifice self. See Rise Goes Up Book One and Two.

Thus, the Book of Malachi is wrong – false.

Michelle Jean
July 07, 2020

IN MY VIEW

In all that is happening here on Earth, God did not cause it. We as humans created this mess then expect God to swoop in and fix our mess for us.

As humans, we do not see our own faults.

We truly do not care. It is only when things get critical, we are calling out to God for help.

We do not stay the course of life yet, expect life to save us all the time from our misgivings, and misdeeds.

We are not fair to God yet, expect God to be fair to us.

We disrespect life yet, expect life to respect us.

We have not put anything into life – God yet, expect Life – God to be our backbone.

Evil is a curse thus, we are the ones to curse self.

We/humans are the ones to follow evil unto our/their death.

Life isn't evil. It is us as humans that bought evil into the picture; our life.

We were told, "the wages of sin is death," but in all many and or, we all as humans do, we forget; ignore the truth. We also ignore the cost of 1 sin – the wage (pay) of one sin.

We say God destroy when God cannot destroy. It is us as humans that have and has destroyed this planet, our life, and the life of others.

See the garbage we dump in the waterways of life.
See the chemicals that are dumped in the waterways of life.
See the way we overpopulate the Earth.
See the many concrete jungles we live in here on Earth.
See the Wars of Death throughout the ages, and centuries.
See the different wars of today including the different conflicts.
See Climate Change.

See the way we cut down the trees of life without truly replanting what we've cut down. Deforestation

See the erosion of Earth's soil due to the different chemicals' humans use to plant, wells we dig, the raping of Earth's minerals, and mineral deposits, manmade lands, and more.

See the genetically modified waste – food humans consume globally.

See human greed
Human strife
Human hatred
Racism

Religious injustice
Political injustice

The unfair laws designed and implemented to break nations.

See the blame game humans play

See the unfair and unjust way we treat self and others, and more.

So, the demise of humans is truly not due to God, but due to humans.

WILL

Therefore, some use their Will for evil instead of using their will to preserve life.

Life is granted to all. It is virtually all that take their life from life - God then believe in lies when it comes to God - the True God of Life. Therefore, if you do not Bank with God, how can God save you?

If God is not your grocery store, how can you eat - God feed you?

If God is not your good soil and good farmland, how can you plant good, or reap good food?

If God is not your good and true hospital, how can you be healed good and true?

If God is not your good, clean, and pure waterways and drinking water, how can your soul - body and spirit survive; become clean?

So, if you have absolutely nothing saved with God, and in God, how can God save you?

Your basket with God is empty.

Your Bank Account with God is empty therefore, you have nothing with God yet, you want God to save you from all that is to come. How does that work?

<u>God don't give loans on life.</u>
<u>God cannot loan you life.</u>

God gave us all life, and we as humans were the ones to squander the life that God gave us.

None thought of the consequences of our sinful actions.
None sought true forgiveness for our sinful actions.

The life of man; each human is not the Life of God. As humans we do not align our self truthfully with God.

We do not seek truth, or the Truth of God. All we do is believe the lies of the bible.

We believe in the lies of religion.

We accept the lies of religion and say, these lies are of God when we of our self know that God is True Life.

Evil cannot tell the truth. Thus, we listen to evil tell us about life as well as, believe the lies these Men – Wicked and Evil Demons tell on God. See man's so-called holy bible.

All who wrote this book – man's so called holy bible cannot escape their judgement because, they are already judged. This I know for more than a fact.

God cannot lie because the truth cannot lie.

Yes, I doubt God at times, get down on God, but God cannot say I did not make Him and or, Her God my Beating Stick, Doubting Stick in All.

God is my true all therefore, God is whom I go to, lash out at, quarrel with, complain to for all.

Yes, I need changes in my life, and I am making those changes. Yes, I still have sin on my docket, but in all I do, I am hoping that God let one of my good outweigh 1 (one) sin if not all of my sins. (1 good outweighing all my sins.) Yes, it is my hope and desire for this to happen. God allowing 1 (one) good to outweigh my sins not just for me but for the Good and True, and truly trying to be good in life, and the Good and Trues Seeds God has and have given me to plant **_only._**

I need my planting to be good, true, clean, accurate, ever growing good, positive, and more good, and true things.

Evil belong to Death so yes, let Death fully and truly take their wicked and evil own on a massive scale.

Life can no longer reside with or, be beside Death's Own come on now.

Life and Death is truly separated in the Spiritual Realm, and so it should be here on Earth.

Good and Evil can no longer cohabitate with each other here on Earth, and I truly hope God listen to me; hear me and make this so – truly separate Good and Evil here on Earth.

Absolutely no one have to live by the White Man's Way – Death's Way.

Life is truly worth it. It is us as humans that take our worth, and self worth from God then complain about it. Therefore, it's time to get rid of all the negatives, negative forces, and negative energy that is plaguing Earth, and the True People; Children and People of Life here on Earth.

Evil must be contained, and be sent back to the Domain of Evil – Death.

Earth can no longer house evil come on now.

Evil destroys
Evil kill

Evil make your life unclean
Evil make you unclean
Evil make your home unclean

Evil make you sin

There is absolutely no goodness in evil.

Evil is hard to get rid of once evil has entered your life.

God do try to save us from evil. It is us as humans that truly do not want to be saved.

Some find it hard to give up what they have – their wicked and evil ways.

Michelle
July 08, 2020

Lovey, with Malachi – the Book of Malachi being the last book of the old testament of man's so-called holy bible. What is going to happen in regards to man's New Testament?

We cannot continue on in lies Lovey.

We cannot let the Lies of Men – the lies of their bible continue on. We have to put an end to it all – the lies of man's so-called holy bible, and man them self.

There cannot be a New Testament of lies Lovey. Thus, truly void man's so-called holy bible – Book of Lies – Death.

Humans can no longer live and die by, and in lies Lovey come on now.

Humans have to know the full truth. We need to tell them the truth.

Yes, these books, but how effective are these books Lovey?
How many know about these books?
How many can get access to these books?

The old is complete; done, let the Lies of Men – Man stay done.

It is time for truth to rise – live good and true – clean. So, let it be truly done when it comes to the Lies of Men.

The Lies of Men have and has destroyed many Lovey, therefore, lies cannot carry on or, continue to conquer come on now. Lies kill Lovey, and the Lies of Men – Man must/have to stop now.

The Lies of Men can no longer dominate Earth. 24 000 years is done – over, let it continue to stay over; done Lovey.

The life and time of Death cannot be extended Lovey.

The Sins of Man – humans have gone on for far too long.

Death can no longer conquer.

Death have to/must go with their wicked and evil own.

Death can no longer prey on life here on Earth. Therefore Lovey, it is wise to let Death go to their domain with their wicked and evil own never to ever return to Earth because, all sin is over; done.

Man – humans – those truthful ones that are of life who remain here on Earth cannot corrupt self ever again.

Evil can no longer use us, and our books; knowledge to rob and steal; deceive Lovey come on now.

Evil must never ever gain access to our knowledge ever again Lovey come on now.

As for us, we need to build anew.
We need to build honest and true.

We need to build good, positive, clean, ever growing clean, good, positive, honest more than continually.

Let truth govern truthfully, honest, pure, positive, good and clean all the time Lovey come on now.

Let no place be found here on Earth for unclean things, unclean people, unclean living, unclean creatures, unclean beasts, unclean spirits, unclean energy, unclean teaching - education, unclean finances, unclean families, unclean children, unclean sex, unclean music, unclean technology, unclean movies, unclean videos and video games, unclean food, unclean planting, unclean growth - growing, strife, war, confusion, and more Lovey come on now. Earth need to be cleansed of all evil come on now.

New Earth
Clean Earth
Good Earth
Positive Earth
Ever expanding Earth

Our Ark - True Ark cannot have anything unclean in it, or on it Lovey come on now.

Michelle Jean
July 2020
Edited July & August 3, 2020

IN MY VIEW

In my view Lovey.

Let me see good things
Hear good things
Know good things
Listen to good music
Listen to, and acknowledge good and true counsel
Grow positive and good seeds
Plant good and true with you always
Live a positive and clean life with you

Lovey, we need a New Earth therefore, we need to get rid of all the negatives, and evils that plague Earth, and I've told you this already. Earth cannot continue in her current state of war and confusion, unhealthy and dysfunctional living by humans.

The lies of humans must come to an end.

Humans have and has caused all on Earth to be corrupt and defiled as them.

Earth truly do not have any moral or true moral values anymore due to humans; human lies, human disobedience, human sins.

Life is good Lovey so; we need to preserve good and true life for our good and true only but, the way Earth is now, it doesn't look as if we can preserve good and true life here on Earth.

We also need to stop the different races from using our knowledge to do evil; deceive, and kill. Our knowledge is right Lovey therefore, evil can no longer get access to our knowledge, and use it for their evil and wicked agenda Lovey come on now.

If it is possible to preserve good and true life here on Earth Lovey, we cannot preserve life, or good and true life for evil. You and I know the damage of Evil therefore, we cannot, and must never ever without end allow evil back into our life again.

I've told you, we need impenetrable frameworks and foundations Lovey therefore, you need to be, must be, have to be our true strength, frameworks and foundations that no evil can penetrate when it comes to us – our good and true own.

We need your true shield of protection surrounding us, and in us that no evil, or negative force, or people can rock us, turn us, or make us doubt you Lovey.

The good and true – our good and true own must never ever give up life for evil; death ever again.

We as your people – true Children and People must truly love you, and truly love self.

We must truly love.
Must truly love. Allelujah

IN MY VIEW

We must truly build each other, and you Lovey good and true.

We cannot build faulty.
We cannot build on belief.
We cannot build on indecision
We cannot build unclean

We have to, must build all on truth, true peace, true honesty, cleanliness, true harmony, truly positive, true truth.

We must forever ever grow good and true without end.

We have to, must build just and be truly just in all that we do.

Lovey, we must bank our Goodness and Truth in you also so that our goodness can collect good interest – grow in all that we do.

Our goodness and truth cannot stop Lovey therefore, Earth must grow good and true all the time.

Earth must void all her evils.

Earth cannot, and must never ever without end allow any form of evil in her again.

Her garden: the Garden of Earth must now be closed off from all aspects of evil from generation unto generation, from everlasting unto everlasting without end.

Lovey, our New Testament must be clean, and void of all evil.

Our New Testament must be positive, clean, be true growth that is built on, and framed out of more than everlasting truth, cleanliness, goodness, the good and true you Lovey that is ever growing, moving, and void of all evil, negative energy, negative growth, negative life, and deceit.

No evil must be in our New World – Testament Lovey come on now.

Life do not need to grow negative.
Life need to grow true – clean.
Life need to grow positive, and unflawed.

Lovey, Man write dirty – unclean with you, but I have to write clean, good, true, truly honest, ever growing good and true; positive with you.

I do not need all the evils of the world with you Lovey.
I do not need the negative forces of life with you Lovey.

The old is done. Let the new be truly clean Lovey.

The damage has been done here on Earth by evil Lovey. You see the nastiness – dirtiness of Earth.

I truly do not need the now, and past filth of Earth in our New Life, and Beginning with you here on Earth Lovey come on now.

No more pain and suffering, no more health issues; woes, no more financial woes, no more greed, no more sin allowed Lovey. This is our new and true beginning with you.

I need you to be my good food, true clean drinking water, good, true, positive living, good, true, positive health, good, true growth, good, true, positive sex, good, true, everything.

Lovey, I see the faults of this world based on human values including my faults; the faults of self, and I truly do not need the faults of humans, or myself moving forward with you.

We can no longer be flawed in life Lovey therefore, this new beginning must be good and true – clean.

Michelle
July 2020
Edited July and August 2020

Let this be the true end of all evil – negative things everywhere Lovey.

Our New Beginning cannot be, and must never be the continuation of evil.

Our New Beginning must be truth, and the continuation of goodness and truth.

Lovey, how much do I complain to you?

So yes, it would be truly nice for me to live fully without so much complaint from me.

Lovey, I need to be on the same page truthfully, and honestly with you.

I need you to truly listen, hear, see, and read these writings.

I need you to correct my flaws – errors also.

Come on Lovey, you cannot be further in time anymore.

Our time must be the same; cannot change or have different time zones.

Physical Time, and Spiritual Time must be the same; one once all evil has and have passed away.

No Lovey, it's not fair, just, or right for you to be separated from us in that way due to sin.

No more Sin and Sins Lovey.
No more living to die.

We must live to live honestly – truthfully.

"The Wages of sin is death Lovey, but Truth is everlasting life."

I need truth therefore, I need good and true, clean and pure honest, just, everlasting life for me, and the good and true seeds you've given me Lovey.

I need truth for our true own, and those who are truly trying to be good despite the obstacles in their way Lovey come on now.

Michelle
July 2020

IN MY VIEW

Things are not right with me Lovey.

I feel as if I am going backwards instead of forward with you.

I feel as if I am stuck in the same place with you where I am held captive – a prisoner with you.

Death is around me again, and I am arguing with Death. Why?

I thought I had indefinitely shut this particular dead down more than infinitely, and indefinitely more than forever ever without end Lovey.

Lovey, why is he still reaching me?

Why can't I shut death down from reaching me?

Why is Spiritual Death so powerful here on Earth Lovey?

Yes, sin I know, but why me Lovey?

What does he continually find me?

I need him; this particular dead to be truly shut down so that he cannot reach me Lovey come on now. I refuse to save him. The damage is done, and I refuse to save my enemies period Lovey. So yes, I truly refuse to save him. He is truly not apart of my saved, and true saved.

Lovey, why can't my life constantly grow up positive, true, rich, truly blessed without all the negatives that surround me, as well as come into my life?

Why do I have to feel as if my life is a prison with you Lovey?

Why can't my world – life be debt free?

Why do I have to incur so much debt here on Earth?

Why can't Earth be a happy place for me, where I live in true peace and harmony with you, and nature?

Why do I have to see the failings of Earth Lovey?

I am falling
Failing

Why does everything have to be so corrupt here on Earth Lovey?

Why does good life have to fail?

Why do evil have to sabotage those who are trying to do good?

I don't know but I do, and at times don't want to know therefore, my life need to be consistent with life; you Lovey.

My life have to be true Lovey come on now.

I truly do not like the inconsistent – yo-yo lifestyle with you.

No one should live a yo-yo lifestyle with you here on Earth, or anywhere for that matter Lovey.

Life is about truth not lies so, why can't we live true here on Earth?

Why do good – those who are trying to do good have to fail here on Earth Lovey?

Why do evil attack good – do all to kill goodness?

Michelle
July 09, 2020
Edited July 31, 2020

IN MY VIEW

I don't want to care anymore Lovey, but I have to.

I don't want to feel anymore, but I have to.

I don't want to see anymore, but I have to.

I don't want to die, and I don't have to.

I need to be free from the restraints of you Lovey.

Your prison walls are not mine. Truly not fair to me.

Yes, I am listening to *PRISON WALLS by Jah Cure.* Therefore, I need you Lovey without the walls.

My life is hard at times. Therefore, I need to tear down the walls that cage me.

I so need a positive and true change in my life.

I truly need a better way in life Lovey yet, you can't see this.

You can't see that many are hurting at the hands of evil; the corrupt.

Lovey, how can we rely on you if you are not truly hearing our cries?

How can we rely on you Lovey if, we cannot connect or, truly connect to you?

Yes. I know billions are not yours – have their name in the Book of Death and not in the Book of Life. But those who are truly trying to secure their life with you Lovey, truly secure us so that we do not fail self, or you.

If you truly trust us, truly love us, then truly save us. Truly save us from the Earthly and Spiritual Demons that surround us as well as, keep us captive so that we cannot rise or attain true life with you Lovey.

The tears Lovey.

The tears because I do cry to my living, financial woes, health woes, family woes, and more at times.

Therefore, we need hope Lovey.

We need you to save us.

We need you to ordain a true place, and space for us here on Earth with you if possible. The sins that are consuming Earth right now Lovey. But, if possible, ordain a true, and clean space/place for me, you, our chosen few only.

Therefore Lovey, stop erecting walls that cage us. Meaning, it's time we do all to stop Evil from consuming Good.

We need to shut down – collapse all the walls that hinder us from reaching our true potential.

We are not animals Lovey come on now.

Life isn't about poverty and pain.

Life isn't about hate, war, strife.

Life isn't ill.

Life, true life grow yet, for the good and true – those who are trying to be good, our life is stunted – cannot grow the way we need it to grow, and this is truly not fair.

We need a true change Lovey.

Earth need a true change for the better good of our own and not evil Lovey come on now.

Michelle
July 09, 2020
Edited July and August 2020

Earth is run like a Whore House.

Why Lovey?

Now I ask you. Where is your domain here on Earth?

Can you even have a domain here on Earth given the nastiness that outline, and fill the Earth?

Where is the balance, and fairness of justice given Earth is run on unfair laws, and unclean practices?

Why even fight?

No, you Lovey do not fight. But change come from within.

Now I ask you this Lovey. Does Mother Earth want, or need true change for her?

If so, she need(s) positive change for self.

When is she going to start changing herself for the better good?

When is she going to evict all the evils from her?

Michelle
July 09, 2020
Edited July 31, 2020

Lovey, what do you truly want and need out of Earth?

Why is Earth so important to you given the unclean state Earth is in?

Everything around me is death.

Why can't everything around me be true and positive life Lovey; growth?

Why is my sight not solid with you Lovey?

Why is my sight distorted at times?

Confusion is not right Lovey.
Confusion is truly not right.

Yet, the cages we are in here on Earth.

Physical Cages
Spiritual Cages

How do I escape these cages Lovey?

The circumference of Earth according to man is 40 075 km, but for years the measurement of Earth has been bothering me Lovey. The measurement of Earth bothers Earth also.

No human can measure Earth Lovey this I know for a fact without doubt. If man could measure Earth, they would know the end of Earth.

They would know Middle Earth – the Middle of Earth.

Now tell me Lovey. How did man come up with this false figure to define Earth?

If man knew the true distance from end to end of Earth, then man – humans would fall out of Earth. Thus, man – humans would know their end – the End of Time.

Oh Allelujah.

Lovey, there is no distance to Earth in that way because, Earth hath no end distance wise in that sense – human terms. And Mother Earth, forgive me if I explained you wrong distance wise. But Earth hath no end distance wise.

Michelle
July 09, 2020
Edited July and August 2020

Lovey, if we are not educated on life truthfully, how will we know how to live truthfully?

If we know not the truth of life Lovey, how will we know you?

If you do not educate us on you Lovey, how are we to know you?

If life begets life Lovey, why isn't all life here on Earth good?

Why do we have monsters, hogs; all form of evil here on Earth Lovey?

When is life comforting Lovey?

When will it all change for the better good of our good and true own only Lovey?

Michelle
July 10, 2020

Lovey, the Book of Life is the Book of Life.

How can anyone uphold life here on Earth if the life here on Earth is not truly clean?

In all I write Lovey, what say you when it comes to life; our New Life here on Earth?

Negative cannot grow positive. Negative can only make all dirty - unclean.

Negative stunt your growth when it comes to life - true life.
Negative kills.
Negative destroys.
Negative void your life with God.

Therefore Lovey, we need to get rid of all the negatives of Earth so we can live true.

I know the worst is yet to come weather wise.
This is the calm before the storm weather wise.

Death - White Death dressed in Black is building - building up current in the sky - far up, and it's only a matter of time before destruction hit Earth.

I dreamt - seen Earth being decimated. Now to see Final Death - White Death dressed in Black laying electrical wires that all connect. Wow

Which lands that is going to lay in total ruin I truly do not know Lovey. But this weather calm is beyond me. A bit eerie for me, but truly do not scare me though the feel is truly eerie.

Yes, you can feel and smell the weather, but the weather is truly elusive - cannot be controlled by any human.

Spiritual weather patterns cannot be tracked therefore, true destruction of land that are void of water - hurricanes cannot be tracked - traced.

Michelle
July 2020

Therefore Lovey, humans are the worst disasters to live.

Humans do destroy it all without truly thinking of the environment we live in.

For many, Eco Living. But, Eco Living for the many are resorts – money for them, not the preservation of the environment.

Money must be made thus; the Trees of Life are sacrificed in the Name of Money – Profit – Human Greed.

Eco Living is not about giving back to the Environment in my view. Thus; human waste, human consumption, human greed.

Humans cannot preserve. Humans can only destroy – kill.
Over produce – kill.

Thus, in my world with you Lovey, our good and true people must preserve good and true. We must respect the environment.

We must plant what we need only.

We must consume what we need only.

We cannot overproduce.
We cannot, must not overeat.

We must plant truly organic – void of all harmful chemicals.

We must be balanced, and in harmony with nature.

Our knowledge base in furthering our environment must be truly true Lovey therefore, truth must always be with us as well as, goodness.

Our foundation now Lovey must be good and true.

Michelle
July 11, 2020
Edited August 2020

IN MY VIEW

In our land Lovey.

The soil cannot erode.

The Sun cannot eat the grass of our lands.

The Sun cannot stifle – do all to wither and kill our Trees of Life.

All must be balanced and harmonious weather wise.

The Waters of Life we need Lovey. Therefore, the Waters of Life must water our lands thus, harmony – balance weather wise in our lands.

Further Lovey, I know the Energy of Life that is out there.

Can we not use this energy source to separate Good from Evil here on Earth?

Lovey, I truly need to talk to you truthfully about this energy source.

As Spiritual Evil is separated from the Good of Life in the Spiritual Realm, we need this true separation here on Earth when it comes to the Good of Life, and Satan's true own – Evil.

No hurricanes are allowed to devour our lands Lovey.

Showers of rain we can have. These showers must clean the Earth – soil, cleanse our lands when the lands need cleansing.

Our drinking water must be separate from our bathing water Lovey come on now.

Rivers, Streams, Waterfalls, Lakes we must have but, our drinking source must be separated from all other sources. Spring Water to drink must be in abundance in our lands Lovey.

Michelle
July 11, 2020
Edited August 1, 2020

Our mode of transportation must be truly different.

Hover cars that are not fueled by oil we must use.

We will design true, clean transportation for our people Lovey including flying cars.

I know it can be done therefore, our people must be true innovators that think of you, and the environment all around them; us.

Lovey, you too must help us create truthfully, pure, harmoniously.

Further, there is something I am missing about Earth.

Lovey, with me wanting and needing Evil to be separated from the Good of Life. Can we not create lands that are truly different from the lands evil live in?

So, for example, you've deemed Jamaica unclean, and I've deemed the United States of America unclean. Can we not create a different land using the great energy that is out there for only our good and true people to live?

And in doing so, if this can be done; for which can be done; can we not cleanse – clean our body, thoughts, spirit from all negative and evil sources?

Lovey, knowledge is not limited in your realm, but here on Earth knowledge wise I truly feel limited. Why?

Lovey, we – our good and true need a good and true environment. So Lovey, I truly do not want or need to build over the garbage humans put in the ground including their dead.

Please Lovey, a New Earth.

New living space void of sin – all humans put in it to destroy the land, and soil.

Michelle
July 11, 2020
Edited July and August 2020

We need a new source of light; life here on Earth Lovey but, how can we get this new light, and life if all access to truth is cut off from me?

If I cannot fully and truly attain you – life Lovey, how can I live good, and true – clean?

How do we remedy all Lovey? Meaning, how do we fix the ills of this Earth?

With all the sins of each individual living and dead Lovey, can Earth be saved?

I do not know the value of 1 good with you Lovey.

You've not shown me the blessings of 1 good, so how am I to know you?

How am I to teach true if I truly do not know all?

What even constitutes goodness in your book, language, day to day living Lovey?

With all the evils here on Earth Lovey, can one good even keep us sane for times time time without end?

Why the split of Good and Evil?

Why not keep all pure?

Why Will – the evil nature of men – some humans that feel the need to control – dominate – cause total chaos of all life?

Why disrupt the harmonial flow of life Lovey?

Why did evil – true evil – all evil have to come into play – physical life of humans?

<u>WORLD STATE</u> – Bushman

<u>LOVE CREATED I</u> – Tarrus Riley

Michelle
July 12, 2020
Edited August 2020

It's July 13, 2020 and my dream world is strange.

Dreamt about the 25 people that got shot in Jamaica.

<u>Dreamt the killings had to do with Visa Fraud.</u>

In the dream, Paula Llewellyn was involved in that she was killed.

Someone shot her but; in the dream, I did not care who shot and killed her along with the other 25 people who got hurt.

I will not analyze this dream because I know Jamaica is run on, and by corruption thus, <u>God did deem the land unclean.</u>

Corrupt Politicians
Corrupt Lawyers
Corrupt People
Corrupt Family Members
Corrupt Cops
Corrupt Judicial System, and more.

In Jamaica your life is truly not valued thus, money talk – can buy you anyone on the island.

The Life of Jamaicans is truly not pivotal when it comes to saving land and people from total destruction. So, I will not worry about a Nation of People that live in lies.

Lie on Life.
Do all to kill self and land.

Have and has taken God from them literally.

Cannot respect their National Anthem or, live by their National Pledge. Therefore, the cost of the Sins of Jamaicans have and has locked country and people out of life – the Life of God.

Jamaicans cannot blame anyone for losing their place – Judah's Place in life apart from them – Jamaicans.

Michelle
July 13, 2020

I do not know who is going to die in my family, but someone is on the Docket of Death.

Muscle spasms is getting the best of me again.

God the pain I am in that I have to swear at times.

I had such beautiful reprieve, and now chaos is back in my life pain wise.

I so need a cure for this debilitating pain that lock up my toes, and fingers at times.

The pain is shit – painful that I can't take it anymore.

Hopefully I get to be in the right environment where I find a cure – true cure for Muscle Spasms.

This pain is worse than the pain of Childbirth, and Gall Stones to me.

When your toes lock up, the pain you are in.

When your fingers lock up it's so hard to unlock them. It's as if you're going to break your bones when you try to unlock your fingers and toes.

Then the leg spasms get to you. Cause such pain that you cannot walk. Using a hot towel, or rag help but lord have mercy to the pain.

Michelle
July 13, 2020

IN MY VIEW

There is so many things happening that I do not know where to begin dream wise.

Dreamt I was in Iceland.

All was well there then I looked up to the west of me in the sky. What I saw was not pretty.

I saw this huge storm of dark gray coming towards me.

I do not know how huge a sandstorm is, or how massive a tornado can get but think massive.

The huge storm broke, and you could see something like a huge hand coming towards the ground.

I scrambled for safety and so did the now Prime Minister of Canada; Justin Trudeau.

In the dream, I was saying I cannot get to safety - fly because I had no passport. I lost my passport in my hustle of trying to get to safety.

In the dream Justin Trudeau's family came into play.

Him Moon Walking - but not Moon Walking, *but modelling it seems.* He was in jeans, white running shoes like Adidas running shoes, and shirt. I cannot tell you the colour of his shirt. All I can tell you is his running shoes and pants - jeans pants of blue.

I do not want to analyze this dream because I am not sure if the dream is related to the movie Martian Land that I watched.

I do not want to put any emphasis on this dream. Therefore, I do not know if Justin Trudeau is going to leave office soon, nor do I know if an earthquake, or tsunami and or, a volcano is going to erupt in Iceland if not a massive snow storm is going to blanket Iceland that see Canada being affected.

When I woke from the dream yesterday - July 13, 2020, I did not put any emphasis to this dream. So, I am going to leave this dream alone.

I just have to watch and see if any thing happens to these lands.

Further, I---you know what; at times though rare - not often you can feel the sting of Death - the dead reach out to me.

John Travolta's wife wow because I felt the sting of Death. Then Konshens brother Delus was holding on to me in Death. Though I did not see Delus in the dream, I know what this dream means.

Death for some is truly not pretty thus, the dead; some that have just died reach out to the living for a saving grace thus, Kelly Preston's death was not normal despite her dying of Cancer as per her family.

IN MY VIEW

Therefore, I will tell anyone to never strive to go to hell because **life is not just physical. Life is spiritual also,** and billions have been deceived by the different Churches, and Organizations of Death.

Some organizations talk about purity.

Some tell you to lay with virgins and have children with virgins. Thus, many think they have virtuous children without knowing, the virtuous children they have are born from adulterous unions.

Thus, billions truly do not know what constitutes adultery here on Earth, and in the eyes of God.

It is when the spirit shed the flesh that many are finding out that they have no life with God. They are hell bound literally. Thus they - the spirit of some cry out for a saving grace. *Therefore, it is truly wise to know your Good Record versus your Evil Record.*

Have more good than sin in the living so that when your spirit shed the flesh you are safe - saved.

No, no one can live a perfect life here on Earth because many evils surround us.

Many claim to be of God who are truly not of God.

Many use God in the name of Religion to deceive others and take their spiritual life from them. Therefore, always be mindful of those who come in the form of Religion professing to be your saving grace, and of God. God do not send anyone in his or her name.

Religion is truly not a part of God. So, God will never use Religion to educate you about him or her. I know this for a fact.

Yes, I speak of the Woman of Zion, but I know why she's in a church, and I am going to leave it at that.

Billions tell you that Jesus died to save you. But know, *God would never ever let any child, or anyone for that matter die to save you, or anyone.* God is not that vicious, spiteful, and sinful. It is humans - the wicked and evil who have all to gain in Death tell you about Jesus dying for you.

Tell me, if Jesus is dead; died on a cross, how can he save you?

How can your life be spared - saved if he's literally dead?

If Jesus died to save you, how come you are still living?

Would you not have died with Jesus also?

Once my spirit is gone; I cannot save you. Meaning, I can no longer petition God for your life. It's impossible. The only thing I can do if my spirit have not ascended to God is, dream you, and caution you if you are going wrong, show you the evils that are/is coming your way, warn you, and more. I cannot petition God for you.

I will forever remind you and tell you that; the job of evil is not to save you, but to kill you. Ensure you have more sin that good so that your spirit – name is put in the Book of Death. So, truly know who teach you, who you have around you, who you drink with, sleep with, marry, walk and talk with, and more.

Michelle
July 2020
Edited August 1, 2020

More young Black People are going to die.

Saw this young Black Person lying face down on the ground. I could see the face of the person. The person's face was not hidden from me. So, yes more death is coming in the Black Race.

Things on Earth is not getting better therefore, technology – man's deathtology is taking shape slowly globally.

Many will be chipped – tagged – tracked.

So yes, more and more humans globally are losing their fundamental human rights to live free, talk free, walk free, and more.

I so do not know why humans want or need others to control them.

I truly do not know why we as humans give so much power and control to our political leaders that give us death in the different areas, and process of life.

Do billions not think of their spiritual life?

No, don't answer that. Humans truly do not think of their spiritual life thus, many are government owned, and religious owned by the different deceiving clergy members of the globe that use God as a pawn – their deceiver.

Some are corporate owned, gang owned, and more.

We know God is truly not a religion thus, billions do all to live as the deceived – even pay to die – die in lies. See Politics, Science – no, not Science because Science hath no conscience. Scientists are the devil's own like the different political, and clergy leaders that use God as their Bitch – well the name of God as their bitch globally.

Michelle
July 2020
Edited August 1, 2020

Therefore, I tell you, Absolutely, no one have to live the White Man's Way – Death's Way.

The White Race is not the prevalent race globally God wise – or in anyway.

Lies is truly not of life.
Greed is truly not of life.
Death is truly not of life.

Therefore, if God is life – true life, then; God cannot die, and will never die.

I know life cannot die because Earth is the Domain of Physical Death; Spiritual Death must commission Physical Death; aide you humans in dying.

Thus, Spiritual Death do come into Earth.

Spiritual Death do command Physical Death – Black Death.

Michelle
July 14, 2020

So, with me knowing this, and you knowing this – Physical Death and Spiritual Death.

Why is it that you Lovey continue to let Evil use you – well your name as their bitch in deceiving billions; humans globally, universally, spiritually, and more?

When are you Lovey going to turn from and or, stop the wicked and evil of the Earth from using your name – God as their weapon to fool, use, and abuse – get billions to sin – die?

Lovey, no evil should say God.

Yes, we say God but for me; Lovey suit(s) me just fine when it comes to you.

It's time for you Lovey to kick all manner of evil off your coattail. Thus, evil should never ever call on you.

Michelle
July 14, 2020
Edited August 2020

Lovey, when did you put humans on Earth to fight amongst each other?

When did you ever say conflict is right?

When did you say; humans because I don't like you, or truly like you, create conflict, fight amongst each other, and kill each other?

When did you Lovey and God become a savage that you don't know how to live?

Lovey, when did Death become your principle, and stay in life?

When did you Lovey become tired and bored of life that you've given up on life; your life, and the life of our Children and People?

When did you start lacking wisdom Lovey?

When did you become flawed?

Michelle
July 14, 2020

Lovey, why is negative energy so strong here on Earth?

No, don't answer that Lovey. I already know the answer.

As humans; we are accountable for our sins – actions here on Earth, and in the Spiritual Realm.

We are the ones to sin and expect to get right for the wrongs we've done.

We as humans are the ones to think we can right our wrongs we've done.

Absolutely no one can right any wrong. All we can do is seek forgiveness from the person we've hurt.

Aye Lovey, I truly miss you.

Speak to me.

Let my sight be truly right because I do rely on my sight – dreams.

Lovey, why is it that humans put so much emphasis on physical life?

Lovey, I see into the spiritual world, know the spiritual death of some yet, people cannot see this. The death of their spirit shortly.

Woe unto man as to what's to come because the Old Testament of Man is done Lovey. Therefore, we must shut down, and truly void Man's New Testament of lies and deceit.

The day – 24 000 of Death is over Lovey. You cannot under any circumstances let evil regain, and reclaim Earth. Death must go – be satisfied with their wicked and evil own and go from Earth so that Earth can renew herself, and cast out – truly lock herself off from all evil. Earth can no longer give Evil access to her. Come on now Lovey.

Michelle
July 14, 2020
Edited August 02, 2020

Lovey, why is it that Death truly do not like what I write?

It's July 19, 2020 and I don't know why Death is creating havoc in my life in the form of old death that I thought was locked in hell and can't bother me via my dream world, and physical life anymore.

I do not know why this death feel the need to want to show up in my life after all these years. Thus, we are constantly fighting – I am fighting with Death.

So sick of it all.

Dreaming America is going to start war.

What is it with this Nation that feel the need to stir up trouble globally?

What is it with them in killing people?

Do they not know God?

No, that was a stupid question on my part Lovey. This nation know not life thus they fight; kill all those who oppose them at will. This nation has no remorse. Thus, America is the killers, and killing field of Death.

Lovey, America – the United States of America is the domain of Death here on Earth.

We as humans allow this evil nation – the United States of America to kill at will without this land – the United States of America being charged for Crimes Against Humanity – all life for that matter.

The Dominican Republic I truly do not know if a hurricane is going to ravage the land, but something is on the docket for this land environmentally weather wise.

<u>Dreamt the now President of the United States and Russia. Donald Trump and Vladimir Putin.</u>
They were someplace – a summit and or, gathering. Donald Trump went up to Vladimir Putin and pulled him aside. It was as if these two were great friends to the way Donald Trump held on to Vladimir Putin.

I cannot tell you what these men said, but in the dream, I was blaming them for something. **<u>I can't remember if it's the war the United States of America started.</u>**

This is not the first time I am dreaming about the United States of America starting War.

You know what I will not worry about the United States of America on what they do globally because every evil nation must fall and the people of that land must pay; suffer the price for the evils their presidents and overseers do.

So, whatever Vladimir Putin and Donald Trump are planning together behind closed doors, it is being seen. Thus, evil will always support evil period.

IN MY VIEW

Just as Babylon fell America – the Eagle must fall – become a wasteland.

Lovey, just as some Black Lands fell in the days of old – America must fall never to rise again. The evils of America; the United States of America outweigh any goodness of the land thus, the negative energy that encompass the land and people literally.

For some, life hath no worth and you Lovey cannot worry about these people; Americans literally.

You have to leave them to the path they have chosen for land and self. America's – the United States of America sins must fall back on them Lovey.

This war that the United States is going to start must consume and condemn; fall back on America – the United States of America and their people wherever Americans are globally. Warmongers must never inherit the Earth, and profit from or off the Earth Lovey ever again come on now. No war is warranted thus fighters of any war are truly not heroes but; murderers that accept pay to kill willingly, and knowingly and you Lovey cannot forgive this anus crime – sin.

It's July 20, 2020 and I got some disturbing news. My uncle on my father's side of the family is not doing so well. I do not know if he is going to live past the end of July. Right now, I just have to hope for the best for him. Have not seen him in decades nor do I remember what he looks like. I never grew up around him, so we are like unto strangers. I would pass him on the street without knowing that he's related to me.

As for my dream world it is so weird. I dreamt Common, Queen Latifah, and Shaquille O'Neil. The dream is so weird that I cannot make sense of it. Common was in the distance. I wanted to get an autograph from him, so I went over to him and asked him for his autograph. He was with this White Female. Suffice it to say, I did not get an autograph from him. He had dirt; garbage in a white bucket with a stick in it, and he wanted me to throw the garbage in the bucket away. I was shocked at what he did, giving me his garbage. Suffice it to say, I did not take his garbage. I left him to throw it out for himself. Refusing to take his garbage out, this boy that was with us said, he Common can go across the street. I cannot tell you if it's to throw his garbage out and or, to park. See Common went into the back of the car that the White Girl drive. He was so bunched up in the car that he could not fit.

Then I was with a younger Common with beautiful Black Hair that was not kinky – unlike Black People Hair. He was handsome and had a gold yellow hue around him. He said he had a brother. His brother was of Norwegian no, not Norwegian lineage but Scandinavian lineage. Common gave me the name of his brother but I cannot remember the name. All I remember is this V with the left side of the V a bit higher than the right side of the V.

After that I saw Common with Queen Latifah. Wow to the way they were going at it kissing each other and getting it on. Queen Latifah now had this beautiful baby with her. The baby began to cry, and she tried to kiss the baby to stop crying.

Weird yes.

After all that I was not with an older Shaquille O'Neil. Tall, dark, and not so chubby. We were talking about taxes. I think I asked him about his taxes. I know he said his taxes are paid up to date, and he did not know why some do not pay their taxes; they leave their taxes to others to look after.

When Shaq said his taxes was paid up to date, I was happy. I hugged him and told him I was proud of him although he was a Free Mason.

He said, he did not like being a Free Mason because he had to make sacrifices. He also said, his dead brother protects him, and they cannot hurt him. He thought his dead brother was saving him from hell.

I wanted to tell Shaq that the dead cannot save you. When you make sacrifices, you forfeit life with God, and you cannot be saved, nor can your children be saved if you have kids. You, and your children belong to death.

No, I will not analyze this dream because there is so many things happening in the dream. I do not know if something is going to happen to Common. If he's going to be in an accident, or if Death is around him literally. You know what let me leave it alone.

Did I dream about the WWE again?

Yes, but I am so not going to worry about the WWE.

Right now, many in America; the United States of America are sacrificed. This many people know but the lid is closed when it comes to these sacrifices. This is truly not my concern. Death have to be paid, and Death is being paid. There are no ands, ifs, or buts about this.

The choice humans make to die is truly up to them. Americans have to pay death. Thus, those who live by the sword must die by the sword.

Those who make human, and animal sacrifices unto death must die.

The land they live in must be consumed due to the debt the land and people has, and have racked up.

There is Life and Death, and Death literally owns billions. There are no ands, ifs, or buts about this. Therefore, the choice of man - humans are the choice, and choices of humans; each individual. You cannot bow down to Death and give Death your all and think God is going to save you. God cannot and will not save you because your interest, and savings, including chequing account was truly not with Life; God for whom I call Lovey.

The job of evil is to ensure all who are of life fail; forfeit life with God, and evil is winning right now.

Death own billions and this is sad, but this is the choice we as humans make for self.

Blacks were to Forfeit Life, and Blacks are forfeiting Life literally. The state Blacks are in globally is more than depressing, but we have to blame our self for the situations we are in. ***We have to learn to let go of the negative past that is affecting us now, and future wise.***

Blacks can no longer fight for, and with Death.

Blacks can no longer keep Death in their lands because Death is killing us literally.

Black Lands can no longer house the Army Bases of Death in their lands. When they (Blacks) continue to do this - keep the Army Bases of Death in their lands they are telling God - All Life that Death is their choice for land, and people. As Mother Africa got rid of some of her wicked and evil own Lovey, Earth must now do the same. Get rid of all the Evil within her literally.

Earth can no longer aide Death in death. She must clean up herself for the better Good of Life - true, good, and clean life come on now Lovey.

Nothing negative can save us. All that is negative keep us chained to negative things; all the negatives that is affecting us individually, and collectively.

<u>*No one can undo the past; we can only live for a better, and brighter tomorrow. Meaning, by letting go of all the negatives in our life, we will begin to heal; live.*</u> Yes, it's hard because many cannot let go. This is them, but you are different, and you cannot look at others when you are doing all to achieve for you.

<u>*The pain you feel in not the team's pain. It is your pain.*</u> **You are feeling it not the team. However, if you have a strong bond with that person, you can feel their pain. But how the world is today, no one feels the pain of people; others because some live to kill, and do kill therefore, they cannot fathom the pain they are leaving the family of those they killed behind.**

Pain doesn't go away that easily for some.

It takes years, decades. For some, the pain never heals. Therefore, no two individual can live the same life. We all have our own life therefore, we have to; must live our life for self. I cannot live your life for you, I can only live my life for me.

Yes, the life here on Earth is crazy for some, but it's them.

Yes, I would like to live in a world were there is no death, confusion, sin, dysfunction, family squabble, children squabble, theft, corruption, and more, but unfortunately, this cannot be because not all desire truth; true life. Some desire Death - are of Death.

Yes, life is different for some. But you know what; I am so not going to worry about the difference in life. There is so much corruption out there that I cannot comprehend some Black Men on a whole.

The way some use our Black Sisters is beyond me. What's the point of having different children with different women that you neglect?

You're not a father but a sperm donor. If you don't want children don't have them. No child should grow mother and fatherless. Some of you think God respect, or look upon you when you have this child with this woman and that woman. <u>God do not favour you because, you disrespect the womb of life period.</u>

Why contribute to the death of self and child; your children?

Millions of children are born through adultery. Therefore, those billions cannot be saved. You knowingly, and willingly did wrong.

It is not of God, nor is it wise to have children for this woman, and that woman. You are bringing sin; condemnation unto your child.

<u>You know what, let me stop because many Black Men are nasty. They cause our Black Women to sin reckless and rude. Therefore, MEN CANNOT BE THE CHOSEN OF LIFE. They can only be the CHOSE OF DEATH.</u>

I am not God, but to the way some men are here on Earth, if I was God, I would chose and or, choose none to carry on life to the nastiness some participate in. Meaning, lock them fully off from life.

Many do lie on you Lovey and yes, some women are no better. They follow in the footsteps of the demons – male demons who defile you Lovey – all life.

When did you Lovey say, whoredom was fine?

When did you say having more than one person in your life relationship wise was fine?

Yes, it's sad that we as humans use each other as sexual merry-go-rounds.

Yes, I am older and wiser therefore, life truly has and have merit to me.

Michelle
July 2020
Edited August 2020

Lovey, it's 1:44 am August 2, 2020, and I have to ask you. *What is the JACK HILL PROTOCOL?*

In the dream, it was a machine – War Machine that George W. Bush – the son commissioned to be built, and used.

In the dream, the Jack Hill Protocol came into play to be used against people.

Which people and or, nation I do not know.

All I know is. The weapon was commissioned to be used on people.

Americans I truly do not know.

Now Lovey, is this machine to be used against China?

I've dreamt twice now that America – the United States of America is going to start the war.

I truly do not know if the war have to do with China, but somehow China was involved but you could not see China in the dream. It was implied.

Now let me ask Lovey. *Is this war the FINAL BATTLE OF DEATH?*

Their – the White Race's Armageddon?

Therefore, I know; there cannot be a WAR OF GOOD AND EVIL. Good cannot, and will never fight against evil on any Battlefield of Death. Thus, this war is evils way of solidifying their place in hell with Death Lovey literally.

I will not go further into this because; you Lovey see, and know the truth of America – the United States of America, and you cannot protect America and her people anymore. The United States of America must go down to hell because they did seal their fate in hell literally.

Lovey, you have to let Israel go. They Israel start conflict – wars with others, build weapons and diseases to kill nations, and each other.

You see and know this Lovey therefore, you have to take your life out of Israel – the United States of America because like Judah, Israel is no more. They Israel – the United States of America is too unclean.

Michelle

Lovey, we can no longer let the Black Race fall victim to their preys (the White Race), and other races – nations.

The New Testament of man's so-called holy bible must be voided Lovey.

Cannot come to realization Lovey.

Blacks can no longer die at the hands of their enemies.

Tell me Lovey. Have Blacks not been crucified enough throughout the ages, and centuries? Have Blacks not been lynched; hanged enough?

Have Blacks not been lied to enough?
Have we not been deceived and abused enough?

Have Blacks not strayed enough?
Have Blacks not died enough?
Have Blacks not been raped enough?

Have our life past, present, and future not been stolen enough?

Have our dead not been disrespected, and robbed enough?

Therefore, it's time to render evil unto evil Lovey.

It's time evil – the wicked and evil of Earth pay. Evil cannot go free Lovey come on now.

We cannot have mercy for the merciless Lovey come on now.

Those Blacks that has and have sided with Death over Life. They too must pay. There cannot be any place in your kingdom, my kingdom, and our kingdom for them. They – those Sell Out Blacks must be truly locked out of life like all Ethiopians, and all Babylonians.

Ethiopia did side with Babylon Lovey. Thus, Ethiopia forfeited their life and until this day Lovey you have a bone to pick with them – Ethiopia.

Lovey, this fight between Israel and Judah including Brazil. Truly safeguard Judah – the land and not the people of Judah if possible. The people of Judah – Jamaica too wicked. They need a true beating but then again, the People of Judah prefer hell hence, they do all to bring them self – lock self in hell – their hell. Thus, absolutely no one can seek, or get forgiveness in dirty clothing.

It's time we stop talking Lovey and start doing truthfully for the betterment of our True Black Own only globally.

IN MY VIEW

STOP TALKING - Fiona

Truly listen to the lyrics Lovey, because our good and true own need us to truly secure a better future for them. *Therefore, we need to Stop Talking and start doing good and true for our good and true own only Lovey.*

Lovey, you truly need to take your life and goodness from all the lands that belong to evil – Death.

Your Waters of Life can no longer preserve the lands and people of Death.

I know the importance of Water – Life Lovey.

Death hath not life so, your waters, rain, and Waterways of Life Death's wicked and evil own should not have.

Billions chose Death for self Lovey therefore, your life should not aide Death's wicked and evil own. So Lovey, step aside and let Death provide water for their wicked and evil own.

Death's wicked and evil own truly do not like you, or truly love you Lovey so you Lovey should not maintain and sustain your enemies globally.

Yes, I write, and it's time You Lovey truly read our words and adhere to good and true counsel.

Read our worlds and truly take you from the wicked and evil of Earth. You did this. Took your life from the Spiritually Wicked. Now it's time to do so; take you from the Physically Wicked here on Earth. Thus, it's time the talking stop, and the true doing begin.

Michelle
August 2020

BOOKS WRITTEN BY MICHELLE JEAN – 2020

FIRST BOOK OF 2020
BOOK TWO 2020
JUST ONE OF THOSE DAYS 2020
TRUTH – THE MONTH OF TRUTH – FEBRUARY 2020 AND BEYOND
ENGLAND – MANKIND
I DON'T KNOW BUT I DO
CANDIDLY SPEAKING LOVEY
THE COMPLEXITY OF LIFE – CONFUSION
2020 SO FAR
THE SPIRITUAL

COMING SOON:

PRAYERS 2020